Surrounded by
Miracles

Surrounded by
Miracles

John Wheeldon

authorHOUSE®

AuthorHouse™
1663 Liberty Drive
Bloomington, IN 47403
www.authorhouse.com
Phone: 1-800-839-8640

Published by AuthorHouse 10/25/2014

ISBN: 978-1-4969-4325-5 (sc)
ISBN: 978-1-4969-4326-2 (e)

http://commons.wikimedia.org/wiki/Category:Heinrich_Hofmann#mediaviewer/File:Christ,_by_Heinrich_Hofmann.jpg

Heinrich Hofmann [Public domain], <a href="http://commons.wikimedia.org/wiki/File%3AChrist%2C_by_Heinrich_Hofmann.jpg">via Wikimedia Commons</a>

Dedication

*For my parents Loren and Hazel Wheeldon;
my wife Susan; children Joe, Sam, Ben, and
Grace; and their spouses Laurie and Chris.*

Contents

Acknowledgements

I would like to thank my sister Nancy Hallenbeck for finding and correcting many of my manuscript errors and Renee Braund for helping with the pictures.

Introduction

Surrounded by Miracles

My life is surrounded by miracles. When I was born my mother Hazel says that the umbilical cord was wrapped around my neck, wrapped around my leg and tied in a knot. They had to call in a special substitute physician three times to help in my birth. Perhaps those three loops could have deprived me of oxygen–my wife would say that explains my strange behavior. But maybe it was a miracle that I was even here at all and God watched over me so I could have the privilege of life here in this wonderful place. The number three seems to be significant in my life. I was the third child. My wife Susan was the third child. I have three sons. I graduated third in my high school class. In I Corinthians 12:28 Paul says, "God hath set some in the church first Apostles, secondarily prophets, thirdly teachers." My parents met as teachers. Two of my sisters were teachers. And I am a teacher.

My sister Nancy dropped me on my head on the concrete floor when I was about six months old. That also helps explain why I'm so strange – you see it's not really all my fault after all!

Perhaps it was when I fell off the scaffold backwards at work and landed on my head on the concrete floor, or maybe in second grade when I fell on top of the slide and broke my two front teeth off and replaced them with gold, or got gassed working at a construction site – any of those things would make a normal person strange. But I like to think it's because I am surrounded by Angels that watch over me and protect me and when the adversary brings harm my way God protects me. Truly I am surrounded by miracles and so are my friends and family.

I felt led to write this little book to encourage you that common people all around you are being watched over by Almighty God and His Holy Angels who cares for us and protects us. He provides for our needs and wants you to know that He is interested in the smallest detail of your life as well as in the concerns of "important" people. Some of these stories are miracles that I have experienced or have heard about in my friends' lives. Some are just funny stories that help make up the fabric of our lives (See Sue and Donna and the chickens).

Mark, Christy, Jenny, and Nancy (dropped me on my head)

1

Finding Work

Working at a job is one of the most important activities for a modern man. It helps each of us to provide for the necessities of life and the needs of our family. In this time of high unemployment in the inner cities of America lack of work is destroying the family structure. Men in particular must work – the Bible puts it so strong in the New Testament that it states if any man not work – let him not eat. Personally I believe the wide availability of unemployment benefits though temporarily of great benefit in the long term are of great destructive power. We must work or we as men lose a part of our necessary male character.

I come from a background where I saw my Dad go to work every day. He sold trailers or "mobile homes" for the Iseman Corporation in Bismarck, ND; Rapid City, SD; and Sioux Falls, SD. It was not a forty hour a week job. He usually was at work by seven in the morning and left at eight at night Monday through Saturday. On Sundays the lot was open in the afternoon. The theory was that if the sales lot wasn't open people couldn't buy trailers and he couldn't sell them to those people.

You might think this is horrible for hours. But this is not that much different from your normal small business man. They put in very long hours so they can have their own piece of the American Dream. There is an equation you might want to know:

(Long Hours) X (lots of effort) = Financial Success

The converse is also true:

(Short Hours) X (little effort) = Financial Failure

In the fall of 1976 I was out of work. I had two small children and my wife was pregnant with our third. We had no insurance. I was looking for work. It was December and the economy was not very good. In September I had been fired from a very good job after I had an accident where my milk truck rolled over. I made it through October and part of November working on an asphalt paving crew but was laid off for the winter around Thanksgiving. Our child was due by the end of December and I was getting desperate.

Every day I would go out and apply for jobs, check back at places I had been before and pray for work. I was driving down Mount Rushmore road in Rapid City and reached the stop light on Omaha street. When I was at the light a Voice spoke to me and told me to go to the civic center. It was the same Voice that spoke to Elijah as a still small voice, not as an audible voice, but a voice in my heart or head – I don't remember which. I went to the civic center job site. I had applied there a week or so before for a laborer's job. That morning by "coincidence" one of the men didn't show up and I was hired in his place. I became a night watchman.

Now there are a lot of strange details that go along with this strange coincidence. First of all – it wasn't at the civic center. Somehow I was confused and this job site was actually for the new Rapid City Central High School. God spoke to me and told me to go to the wrong place knowing that I had the job site confused.

I didn't really enjoy this job much. I would work for twelve hours – 7:00 pm to 7:00 am Monday through Friday and another watchman and I split shifts on the weekend where one of us went 7:00 am to 7:00 pm and the other went 7:00 pm to 7:00 am. It totally messed up my sleep habits. My wife used to have to hush up my two little boys during the day because that's when I slept so I could work all night. We also split the days Monday through Friday so it seemed like we only worked about 48 hours a week. It was kind of scary working at night with the wind blowing the plastic at a lonely construction site.

BUT GOD GAVE ME THAT JOB AND BOY WAS I THANKFUL!!!

Corner of Omaha and 8th Street in 2014.

Rapid City Central High School 2014.

2

Bread in Answer to Prayer

One thing Christians need to keep in mind is that really bad things happen to really good people. I used to believe that everything as a Christian has a happy ending but it's not so. I was reading a book by Davis Bunn – a great Christian author who gives me significant spiritual insights – when he was describing Jesus at the tomb of Lazarus and where it says, "Jesus wept." He seemed to be expressing how that sometimes Jesus is just there with us during a time of trouble or sorrow. The story of Lazarus ends with Lazarus rising from the dead but oftentimes in our trials, Lazarus doesn't rise from the dead but Jesus is still there with us weeping right alongside us in our time of sorrow.

I believe that we as Christians go through experiences that don't have happy endings and have an element of suffering involved. Read II Corinthians 1-3 and you begin to realize that an effective Christian ministry is based on the experiences (read sufferings) of the minister. It's hard to receive consolation from a minister when you lose a loved one if they never have experienced loss. A person who has never been sick has a hard time feeling for those who are sick.

This is all a prologue to the story of Marylou's grandfather. Marylou is a dear friend of mine who was my Pastor Don Derksen's wife. One of Marylou's ancestor's came over on the Mayflower – Edward Doty. This story will be somewhat my version of what happened rather than exactly what happened. One time Winston Churchill was criticized for including the story of Alfred the Great and the cakes in His History of the English Speaking People. Alfred was fleeing after having lost a battle with the invading Danes and was baking some cakes for a peasant woman. He was preoccupied with his troubles and burned the cakes and the peasant wife beat the Great King with a stick. He later won a great battle. Some critic didn't think it really happened, but Churchill loved that story and told the critic that it was HIS version of the History of the English Speaking People—and that's why he included the story or legend of Alfred and the cakes.

I am not suggesting that this story didn't happen. I have heard the story from Marylou several times and in our circles we value the truth above all. I just may have some minor details of this story and some of my later stories wrong. Marylou's Grandfather was a very godly man who was a gifted inventor. He came up with a version of the combine that had never been built before and went to sell it to one of the major farm implement manufacturers. When he was in the manufacturer's office his briefcase with the drawings and plans were stolen and never recovered. A short while later someone else came out with a very similar design. That's the part that's sad because it doesn't have a happy ending. I don't think he ever got the wealth he deserved in this life, he just lived out his Christian testimony the best he could.

He had been planning on money from the sale of those plans to get home and had no money so he hitch hiked. After several days he was tired and very hungry and in great need. He cried to the Lord for help. Just then a bread truck drove by and two loaves of bread fell off the truck. The same God that fed Elijah by the ravens fed Marylou's Godly Grandpa with two loaves of bread!

3

Uncle Fran Goes to Heaven (Almost) and Comes Back

My family is rather eclectic in its religious diversity. My father Loren was Lutheran mostly because his mother Elvina Isaksen was a Norwegian Lutheran. I don't think the Wheeldons were notably religious although we believe the first Wheeldons came over on William Penn's second ship in 1682 and William Penn was a noted Quaker. My father met Hazel Hershey when they were teaching at the School for the Blind in Gary, SD in 1940-1942. The Hersheys were Methodists and Mom had graduated from Dakota Wesleyan University in Mitchell, SD where her family knew George McGovern, the 1972 Democratic presidential candidate.

Dad as a good Lutheran went to Augustana College in Sioux Falls, SD. My second sister Nancy went to Augustana but is a Methodist. Her oldest daughter Jenny is a United Methodist minister that we are all very proud of. Her next daughter Christy is attending Luther Seminary in St. Paul,

Minnesota and will probably be a Lutheran pastor. (I wonder if the two sisters will ever exchange pulpits!)

My youngest sister Alice lives in Kansas City, Missouri and attends World Revival Church which was founded by Pastor Steve Gray who has a remarkable international ministry. Alice is a gifted musician and has four beautiful daughters (one married to my best friend Glenn), and four grandchildren. I'll probably work in some of her trials and tribulations later.

Then is my family. I was raised a liberal Methodist. I became a Jesus Person in the 1970s and have since followed the teachings of Reverend William Branham. Two of my sons are Catholic. My daughter attends an Evangelical Free Church. My son Ben is a beautiful Christian. As I said – we are a very eclectic family – Lutheran, Methodist, Pentecostal, Evangelical, Catholic, etc. – but we love each other very much.

I purposely left out my older sister Laurel because that is where Uncle Fran fits in. Laurel followed mom to Dakota Wesleyan. Wesleyan is a tiny school of about 600 students in Mitchell, SD which is more famous for the Corn Palace. When you go to the Black Hills to see Mount Rushmore you should stop at Mitchell to see the Corn Palace. (As an aside here are the things a tourist needs to do traveling across South Dakota on interstate 90.) People shop in Sioux Falls, see the Corn Palace in Mitchell, get a piece of pie at Al's Oasis at Chamberlain on the Missouri River, take the badlands loop at Kadoka, go to Wall Drug, then stay in Rapid City.

In the middle 1960s Dakota Wesleyan was recruiting Catholic kids from the East coast to go to this little liberal arts school in South Dakota. There were kids from Long Island and one football player from western Massachusetts named Francis Nimmons — Uncle Fran. Uncle Fran hated school. He is the kind of kid teachers dread. He and his buddies picked up a Volkswagen and brought it inside his high school and drove it down the hall. Two of his friends who were identical twins faked falling out of a third story window. One of the twins had run down below while the other twin hung on outside the window. When the female teacher looked down below she saw the other twin all broken up on the ground below and about had a heart attack.

He was the quarter back of the football team but a terrible student. I believe the U of Mass wanted him for football but his grades were too bad. He went on to a prep school named Brewster Academy where three of the guys he played with played pro ball. One of the guys was named Milt Moran. After Vince Lombardi left the Green Bay Packers he coached the Washington Redskins. Uncle Fran wanted to get into the locker room to see Milt but Lombardi didn't let him.

Fran signed up for the marines but his Dad Al talked him into going into college instead. Al Nimmons had this gentle way of asking you to do him a favor and you couldn't tell him no. After Brewster Academy Fran came out to Dakota Wesleyan and was the noseguard on the team. My sister Laurel was one of the cheerleaders. Fran is one of those guys with tremendous common sense and street smarts. He is funny. He is loyal to his family. Don't ever cross him or hurt his family. His dad was English with a gentle disposition. His mom was a short Italian lady and a spitfire.

One time his mother's brother-in-law hit her. His father Al, who I remember as being this reasonable gentle guy, had been a boxer. He took his brother-in-law and pow—pow—pow just about knocked him out. You didn't do that to Al's wife Phil.

Another time to illustrate the passion in Fran whom we all love so well – he had dear neighbor friends Gee and Jerry whose daughter was brutally murdered. It seemed as though everyone knew who did it but the law was helpless. Fran offered to help Jerry go and blow the guy away but Jerry said they couldn't do that because he wasn't sure. You may not understand that feeling but as a father of a beautiful daughter I perfectly understand that feeling.

Fran is a ROMAN CATHOLIC. He knows that because that's what it says on his dog tags. They asked him in the 1960s what to put on his tags and be sure to get it right and that is what they put on it.

Now this is the story of how Fran almost went to heaven. He needed to have heart bypass surgery. Days before the surgery he was in the cardiac catheterization lab when he coded from a dye that is no longer in use. Fran told me that they say that people don't really see the white light and all but he saw the white light. Then it was like he was going through fields. (I thought of the scene in Gladiator where Russell Crowe is going to the Elysian Fields of Mythology and he is going through wheat or barley). Then it was like there was a hill and Fran knew that his love ones were on the other side – but Laurel needed him. So he came back to us.

I'm glad he did.

Fran and Laurel

4

Sue and Donna and the Chickens

My son Joe and his wife Laurie are into natural foods. I'm sure each generation reinvents healthy eating, sex, how to save money, raising children, etc. In Joe and Laurie's case they live in the country and tap maple sugar trees, and get all kinds of wonderful healthy products from neighbors that aren't easily available to the rest of us. Laurie loves natural things: honey, babies, nature, having children at home, etc. She would have fit in well in the late 1960s and 1970s when I was much younger.

Sue and I did many natural things earlier in our marriage. One of our first experiments was with tomatoes. We had about ten tomato plants in some church friends' garden, the Koches. One night in October or September of 1974 there was going to be a frost so we harvested about 10 shopping bags full of tomatoes and Sue canned tomato sauce or paste or something. Did I mention my son Joe was born October 5, 1974!!! Things must have been hectic for somebody because I was working 50 hour weeks at Plains Manufacturing and riveting grainsides until my hands went numb at night. Oh the glories of manufacturing jobs! (Have the people that glorify factory jobs ever worked in a factory 50 hours a week?)

After the great tomato experiment came the raw milk and yogurt experiment. We would find dairy farmers that sold unpasteurized milk. The theory is that pasteurization kills all the good stuff in milk and unpasteurized whole milk is better for you. I worked at Gillette Dairy for a while and if you saw what came out of the filters from the raw milk you might have some second thoughts about "natural" products.

We would take the unpasteurized whole milk and put it in Sue's pressure canner and make 4 quarts of yogurt out of one gallon of unpasteurized milk. I loved that yogurt. I would add some brown sugar to it and eat it at lunch. The guys on my construction crew at Rapid Plumbing used to kid me something terribly about it. "Hey John, have you been to the outhouse yet to get your lunch?" or one day when I was passing gas that was particularly potent George Maher my foreman told me I was either going to have to change my diet or my wife.

Perhaps our best dietary experiment concerns chickens. Sue and I and our friends were raised in town. Our parents were born on farms and moved to town with the exception of my dad Loren who was born and raised in Sioux Falls. Sue had heard from somebody that she could buy chickens cheap out by the airport for like a dollar apiece. She ordered 20 and her friend Donna ordered 10 – how much work could a few chickens be? Think of all those good meals waiting for their husbands and kids in the freezers.

Sue and Donna drove out to the chicken farm. The man talked to them and found out how many they wanted and they said 20 for Sue and 10 for Donna. The man picked up a chicken and wrung its neck. Now us city folk have no idea what that means. It means you grab a chicken by its head and swing it around like a yo-yo in a circle until its body comes off. Then you learn what it means to run around like a chicken with its head cut off. The body doesn't know its dead for a few seconds and so it runs around like a chicken without its head. Then it collapses and gets collected and a shocked Sue or Donna picks up a dead headless chicken and stuffs it into a green garbage bag in the trunk.

Meanwhile John has put in nine or ten hours as a masonry laborer on a construction site. Donna's husband Doug was either working at Robins and Stearns Lumber yard or at Black Hills Power and Light as a lineman. I was dead tired and ready for bed and I didn't lift a finger to help with the birds. Doug was great. Collecting the dead, smelly, birds was the easy part. Doug is an avid hunter and fisherman.

I don't remember the process but the birds had to be defeathered by scalding in boiling water, gutted and cleaned, bagged, and readied for the freezer. As I remember by the time I was ready for work by about 5:00 am the next morning the girls and Doug were just getting cleaned up and ready for bed. We had 20 frozen chickens in our freezer for a long time.

I don't think Sue could ever eat any of them.

5

The Great Rapid City Flood of 1972

ISAIAH 43:1-2 But now thus saith the LORD that created thee, O Jacob, and he that formed thee, O Israel, Fear not: for I have redeemed thee, I have called thee by thy name; thou art mine. When thou passest through the waters, I will be with thee; and through the rivers they shall not overflow thee: when thou walkest through the fire, thou shalt not be burned; neither shall the flame kindle upon thee.

One of my good church friends in Rapid City, SD set Isaiah 43:1-2 to music after her experiences in the Rapid City flood of June 9, 1972. That night changed my life forever. In one night the mighty hand of nature swept away 237 lives, thousands of homes, and caused millions of dollars of damage. Those of us who were delivered from death lost our faith in the power of man and trust in riches to see us through the valley of death and destruction. My father, mother and I escaped the wall of water by twenty minutes.

My sister Alice spent the night praying on the roof of a café as campers, boats, cars, and trucks swirled in the muddy flood waters mere feet from her. It's a little hard to take very seriously the latest antics of the Hollywood or sports world crowd when you are within moments of checking in with St. Peter.

To begin at the beginning. My dad Loren joined the Iseman Corporation in the early 1950s during an oil boom in North Dakota. My mother Hazel and he had worked at the Sioux Falls airbase during World War II training the radio crews for the bombers. Dad had volunteered to join the military in December 1941 but was 4F because his legs were in poor condition because of severe osteomyelitis as a child. As the war wound down he had gotten a job with the Nash Finch company (a grocery wholesaler) and moved to Bismarck, ND.

Mom and dad saved a lot of money during the war because they couldn't spend it during the war. After the war they started to go with a faster crowd and spent more money than dad made at Nash Finch. He then started selling trailers for Iseman and must have done well for those times. By 1962 he was the manager of the sales lot in Bismarck and was offered the job in Rapid City, SD. I was in 4th grade. Laurel was a Senior, Nancy was in 9th grade, and Alice was in 2nd grade.

When we moved to Rapid City there had been a very minor flood in 1962. The Iseman sales lot was on the corner of the busiest intersection in South Dakota. It was on the North West corner. To the south was a nice shopping center called Baken Park. Rapid Creek was a shallow stream that flowed out of the Black Hills to the west of us and then flowed between two mountains known as Dinosaur hill (old timers called it hangman's hill because there was an old snag tree that had been used to hang someone on) and M hill. The gap between the two mountains is called "the Gap". The story I got was that in 1962 Rapid creek overflowed its banks and about 6 inches of water came across West Main and filled up the depression where the Iseman Corp had its mobile homes and ruined the place. My dad was called in to clean it up.

After that, whenever it rained very much, we were very conscious of the weather because we didn't want to get flooded out.

The night of June 9, 1972 was kind of a rainy night. One of my good friends Jim Bickett wanted to run around and do stuff. I was 19 and he was 20. We were both young Christians and we hung around with a lot of other guys our age and just had fun. My mother Hazel had had some kind of a breakdown the previous year and we were rather sensitive and tried to be as helpful as possible. One thing that our Christian leaders emphasized was that children needed to obey their parents and since it was rainy my folks were watching the creek because of the minor flood of 1962.

Jim wanted to go out. My folks wanted me to stay in. I was 19 and actually free to do what I wanted to do but out of respect for them I stayed home. I think the folks and I drove around a little and maybe got a coke or taco and then went home and went to bed. My dad must have stayed up and listed to the tv or radio because they woke me up about eleven o'clock and told me we had to leave. The mayor was just on the news and told everyone on property adjoining Rapid Creek to get out and so we left.

I drove our 1969 Mustang and my Dad drove our 1965 Mercury sedan. We left our used station wagon that I had been driving to college with my blue "Jesus Saves" bumper sticker on the rear. At that time we lived in the Gap where Rapid Creek flows between Dinosaur hill and M hill. Presently there is a soccer field on the location where our trailer once was. (In 1988 my two sons Joe and Sam were part of a team that won the under 12 South Dakota State Soccer Championship on that field)

We left the trailer and spent the night in Robinsdale in the South East part of Rapid City staying with my Dad's fellow employee Kenny. I really hesitate to call Kenny the hired man at Iseman because he was so much more than that. Anything that needed building, Kenny built. Anytime trailers needed to be moved or set up or repaired, Kenny did it. He was a plumber and an electrician and a general handyman. He took us to Sioux Falls in 1969 when Rapid City won the state basketball championship. He was a real friend to our family and when we needed him in 1972 he came through for us and we lived with him when we had no home.

The next morning we woke up and Rapid City had literally been gutted. Fourteen inches of water had fallen above the city in the narrow canyons and killed dozens above the city. Then the water hit Canyon Lake which held a reservoir and burst through the side of the dam without going over the spillway. The Lake sent a wall of water down the flood plain residences. In the gap were a series of poorer trailer parks farther east from where we lived. I was spared the visions of the horrors of that night. I didn't see my loved ones swept away, fires, devastation, trees swirling on the muddy waters. I just saw the aftermath.

Just a few of the personal vignettes—

We found our trailer – the mud was four or five inches deep all throughout. I had put my Bible on my bed which floated up and it was untouched. The picture of Jesus was still hanging on the wall in my parents' bedroom like it had always been.

We dug out our mud encrusted clothes and loaded them in garbage bags. We took them to my mother's cousin Gladys and washed them out in garbage cans. It brought mom out of her depression saving her family. (It bothered me a great deal watching the people during Katrina when I remembered during Rapid City when we lost 237 dead that we didn't wait around for the gubment to help us. We got a lot of help. Uncle Fran's folks cashed in savings bonds to make sure my Dad could keep food on the table. I remember standing in lines to get shots so that when the infected water or insects or typhoid or whatever they were afraid of wouldn't affect us.

One of my swim team friends Gary DeBeer talked about how they would take a line of guys and link arms and walk the creeks looking for bodies.

The missing lists were enormous at first. People didn't know you were safe and since your house and phone were gone you were reported missing. My dad was missing. Then people's names were misspelled. Gradually the casualty lists were finalized at about 237.

One final comment. I don't know if anyone else heard the mayor tell people to get out.

When we later found our trailer it was moved about 6 blocks by the flood waters. The clock was stopped 20 minutes after we left.

6

Alice and the Bookstore

My sister Alice had a Christian bookstore for several years in Jackson Hole Wyoming. She has had some truly outstanding miracles take place before her. You have to understand we are pretty nothings as far as the world goes but God has blessed us so much!

One time she was going over her bills and realized she owed about a thousand dollars. She was coming up on the weekend and somedays her store would only do $50 worth of business in a day. She had about $300 in cash and she spoke out loud "O Lord, I may have miscalculated!"

Just then a man came into the store. He told her, "God told me to give you this."

One, two, three, four, five, six, seven hundred dollars came out.

Alice told him I should be giving to you as you are a missionary.

The man didn't even want her to mention it.

Isn't God great.

Bookstore Sign

Alice inside the Bookstore with Copy of FF Bosworth Book

7

Sometimes It's Okay to Sleep In

In 1994 my mom went to Israel with a Lutheran tour group led by a pastor named Barney. My father had fallen coming in from his car and broken his hip and been laid up for several weeks and urged my mom to go on the trip in spite of his injury. We all knew there was little she could do to help him in the hospital so all my siblings supported mom's trip to Israel.

Mom had a wonderful time.

She promised to take me to Israel next time she went and we planned to go in 2001. In 2001 the Intifida got going in Israel, 911 occurred in New York and it was no longer safe to travel to Israel because of terrorism.

The Wheeldons are from England. We have a geneology book that traces our family back to a Wheeldon that came over on William Penn's second ship in 1682. My mother's mother Daisy Mitchell was of Cornish descent. Her father John Mitchell came over from Cornwall in the 1880s after working in the mines as a boy mining clay. John married

Violet Rundell and settled in Hurley, South Dakota before South Dakota became a state in 1889.

Because of our strong English connections (there is also Scotch/Irish on my mother's side the Livingstons) we decided to go to England instead of to Israel in June/July 2005. Fran, Laurel, my wife Sue, Mom, and I went. We have different views on how to visit places. All have merits. Laurel likes tour guides that know all the local details and shops and restaurants etc. I tend to like to rent a car and blunder around and have interesting adventures. Laurel is really amazed at how things seem to work out for me. I miss a lot of things but I somehow find a lot of things too.

We landed at Gattwick airport and stayed at a little hotel/bed and breakfast around the corner from the British Museum. This is my type of trip!!!! History... History... History.

I need to explain what history is for me. I have a wonderful friend at church named Jamie Stokely. She is very athletic and active and a great person. One day I mentioned to her how much I loved history. She kind of rolled her eyes and got that expression normal people get when they talk to nerds. I know to most people history is some dead stuff you read about in some dry old book. For me history isn't like that. When I am walking on the walls of the Tower of London I'm there with William the conqueror or down in the torture chamber hearing the creak as they turn the gear up a notch on the rack and the victim screams. When I was at the Alamo I could see the line in the sand that William Travis drew that the men crossed over and decided to die for Texas. At Little Round Top at Gettysburg I stood on the very spot where Lawrence Chamberlin, a college professor from Maine stood with a few hundred men of the 20th Maine while James Longstreet hurled the might of the confederate army of Northern Virginia and saved the Union Army.

History is very personal to me. It is courageous men and women making choices that echo down to the present. Our whole trip to England was History. People don't get that about the English. I was really offended at the way President Obama treated Churchill's bust because Churchill represents a great deal of what I see lacking in our society today. He stood alone against Hitler in the 1930s when it was not popular and then was the voice that England needed in 1940 in her hour of desperate need when she stood alone. My mom Hazel got to ride in Churchill's personal elevator at Chartwell his home when we toured it. What a thrill for her!

We got to do so many things. We saw the Rosetta stone in the British museum, used to unlock the mystery of Egyptian hieroglyphics. In the British library we saw the Codex Sinaiticus one of the oldest biblical manuscripts dating to about 350 AD. In the same room is a Guttenberg Bible, one of five copies of the Magna Carta, and the original writing of "Yesterday" by the Beatles.

We saw the Tower of London. Our guide was just excellent. He was a veteran who lived there and very knowledgeable. The crown jewels are okay. As I look back on them I think there are so many that I just get overpowered and they don't seem that special. They aren't something I particularly want or need and I don't really see how they help anybody.

At Saint Paul's church you realize that this magnificent church is less a monument to Christianity and more a mixture of British patriotism and history. In the basement the two greatest British military heroes are interred: the Duke of Wellington and Admiral Horatio Nelson. While we were there remodeling was going on and we couldn't find Nelson's tomb. I asked a man at the information counter where the Duke of Wellington was, and he replied "Oh he is dead – He is very, very dead." The English sense of humor you know.

Eventually Mom and I left on our separate trip. We went to Gattwick airport and rented a car and took off. I had never driven on the left before and that was very interesting but not fatal. Our first stop was Chartwell, the home of Winston Churchill. Mom and I got lost. We probably drove 20 miles out of the way but she actually helped me find the way – an 88 year old and a 52 year old working with poorly marked maps in a foreign country.

Chartwell is magnificent. We ate lunch there. During the 1930s when Churchill was out of power and "alone" he wrote, painted, and actually did masonry work on one of the walls there. Although he spent much of his life there he is not buried there but is rather buried close to his birthplace near Blenheim castle in a small church yard called Bladon.

After Chartwell I wanted to see Canterbury Cathedral because of Chaucer's Canterbury Tales. When we got to Canterbury I was somewhat impressed that the wall appeared to me to be a Roman wall so I left Mom in a parking lot and walked around on the wall and asked about that. It seemed like someone told me that it had been an old Roman camp but I don't clearly remember now. The

Cathedral was enclosed in a wall that we drove through a gate to get within. Remember that the head of the Anglican church is the Archbishop of Canterbury so I believe the See of Canterbury actually heads up the English church. Now I'm not sure how that actually works because it seems that since the time of Henry VIII the English Monarch has usurped the headship of the church so it would seem like the Queen would be the head of the English church.

From Canterbury we went to Dover. On clear days you can see Calais but I don't feel like I could see France. It was getting fairly late at night by now. We were able to see the white cliffs. There is a famous line from a WWII song that goes:

> There'll be bluebirds over
> The white cliffs of Dover

From Dover we drove on to Hastings and stayed at the same hotel that Queen Victoria had stayed in 100 years before. Sometimes when I watch the British mystery 'Foyle's War' I think I see beaches or scenes from the same hotel where Mom and I stayed. In the morning after breakfast we drove about 7 miles north to the small village of Battle where the actual Battle of Hastings took place. In 1066 Harold II king of the Saxons met William I king of the Norman invaders. Harold had just marched in less than three weeks from Stamford Bridge by York about 200 miles to the North where he had fought and beaten off an invasion by the Norwegians under King Harald Hardrada. William had an abbey built on the site of his victory and mom and I toured the site.

From Battle we went to Portsmouth. Originally, I had wanted to go to Portsmouth to see Victory which is the ship from the Napoleonic wars that Nelson sailed on at Trafalgar. But we couldn't get into the abbey at Battle very early so it made me too late at Portsmouth and we got to the ferry for Ouistreham, France just in time. Laurel, Fran, and Sue had taken the train down from London and met us on the ferry. They were getting a little concerned because Mom and I were nowhere to be seen but then we showed up. The ferry ride was very nice and beautiful. The Isle of Wight is in Portsmouth harbor. My Grandmother Daisy had a cousin that lived there whom she corresponded with for many years. It was very picturesque – the sun was setting in the west and we were leaving England behind in midsummer heading from the smooth Portsmouth harbor water into the increasingly choppy English channel.

Sue and I were on the stern of the ferry as the stern began to go up and down – deeper and deeper. Several years ago we had gone sailing with friends from the Neurosurgery lab I worked in during the summer on lake Michigan and were in boat races. One especially choppy race our stomachs were rather queasy and Sue got all the way sea sick and threw up – it's not very pleasant. The English channel is notoriously rough and we had a repeat performance. I was busy for a while rustling up sea sickness bags and disposing of same and trying to find a place of comfort beside the stern which naturally would have the greatest up and down motion of the ferry.

I have a greater appreciation of the opening scenes of "Saving Private Ryan" or "The Longest Day" when the landing craft are hitting the beaches after spending three days in the middle of a storm in the choppy English channel. The men were nervous and seasick and yet went ahead and stormed Fortress Europa. Truly the Greatest Generation. When we toured the cemetery above Omaha beach Mom felt like there were the ghosts of the boys that she had taught at the Sioux Falls Air Force Base during World War II all around us.

We landed at Ouistrehem at sunset which is the port of Caen and took a taxi to our motel in Caen several miles inland.

The next morning I woke up early and anxious. It was my responsibility to have our rental vehicle and I didn't know where the Hertz rental place was. I started walking east – it was about six in the morning and I speak very broken French that I learned in fifth and sixth grade in Rapid City. Many Americans travelling overseas have a funny idea about the French. Somehow they believe that in France the French should speak English. Others believe the French are rude to Americans. This was not my experience.

Early in the morning, in this beautiful French city, the home of William the Conqueror I was walking asking for directions in my broken French. "Direction --- Ce vous plais?"

I walked for an hour or so and finally an older Frenchman gave me a ride the last few miles to the Hertz dealership. God really looks out for me. The French were all very kind to me.

Then I drove the van back to our hotel and we set about site seeing. Our first stop was Pegasus bridge. There Major Howard crash landed four gliders and captured a key bridge from the Germans and held out through the night until relieved by Lord Lovat and his bag piper.

We saw the mulberry port the allies built (an artificial harbor called port Churchill), the Pointe du Hoc where the rangers scaled the cliffs at great loss of life. The shell and bomb craters must be about ten feet deep. I heard that there were collapsed trenches with men buried alive in them. War is a colossal waste of men and treasure. But you never want to lose. Just ask Germany, Japan, or the South. I am a firm believer that we need to have the best. It is criminal to have our men and women go to war with anything less than the best. In WWII we almost didn't have time to make up for the neglect of the 1920s and 1930s. Our torpedoes didn't work, our tanks were inferior and our men were poorly trained and led in the beginning.

We stopped at the town of St Mere Eglise. St Mere Eglise lies behind Utah beach where the 82st airborne came down. Every year they hang a manikin from the steeple to commemorate the paratrooper who was hung up on the church roof and then played dead and survived. When we stopped in the village square Sue went to a small bakery and got a sack full of baked goods. The French eat long loaves that taste great and we shared some good snacks.

We then drove on to the port of Cherbourg where we boarded a ferry for our return trip to Portsmouth.

The next morning we split up again, Mom and I took off and Sue, Fran, and Laurel returned to London. Mom and I started with Stonehenge. Stonehenge is kind of small and just off the freeway. It looks just like the pictures.

Next we went to Glastonbury Abbey. I am somewhat of a Romantic. Glastonbury is the center of Arthurian legend.

Supposedly the bodies of Arthur and Guinevere were found there about 1200 AD and put behind the church altar. A lead plate covered the bones saying that Arthur Rex was buried there. Another legend says that Joseph of Arimathea brought the Holy Grail from Palestine and buried it on Glastonbury Torr. Another legend says that when Joseph landed he planted his staff on Wearyall Hill and it grew into the holy thorn which blooms at Christmas and Easter. Another legend says Jesus was brought by his kinsman Joseph of Arimathea as a young boy and worked in the tin mines in the area. William Blake immortalized that legend with his lines in the British hymn Jerusalem

> And did those feet in ancient time.
> Walk upon England's mountains green:
> And was the holy Lamb of God,
> On England's pleasant pastures seen!

We spent the evening in the city of Bath. Bath is famous for its ancient Roman Baths. Mom and I had supper in a pub but by then I was too tired to seek out the Roman bath.

The next day we drove by Bristol. I had wanted to see the site where George Mueller built his Orphanages by faith and prayer, but I simply ran out of time. On a trip like this there is just too much to see. We could also have gone to Cornwall where my Great grandfather John Mitchell was from but didn't. My next stop was High Wheeldon in the Peaks District North by Manchester. I stopped for directions at a small pub in Buxton and was told that John Wheeldon goes to that pub all the time. At the foot of High Wheeldon (one of the peaks in the Peaks District) is the Wheeldon Trees Farm a small bed and breakfast. Our next important stop that day was by Blenheim castle at the Bladon Church yard where Winston Churchill was buried. Blenheim is where Churchill was born. Bladon is where he died. Chartwell was where he lived before World War II.

When we got close to London on July 5 the information signs above the freeways ominously informed us that London was closed. Mom and I had no idea what that was about. We got to the motel that night and soon found out!!!

Terrorists had attacked London. The Subway and a bus had been bombed.

As the pictures came out they looked sickeningly familiarly. We lodged in a small hotel around the corner from the British museum. We had walked right by the headquarters of the British medical society. Bombing victims were taken to the British medical society. A bus was blown up. I had walked on the street where the bus was blown up. A subway was blown up. I had taken that same subway to Harrods with Sue. In fact that was the subway that Fran, Laurel, and Sue were to take that morning to go on a trip to visit the Burleigh House North of London.

In 2005 we had not yet made the leap to cell phones in our family so we had a difficult time connecting. You can imagine how this was all playing back in Milwaukee, Wisconsin. My daughter Grace was at home following her Senior year in college. She had a friend named Autumn who was soon to be married that was staying with her. We had just made out a will and left it with her and she had heard about the bombings and was a little bit frantic.

Somehow we got connected up with Fran and got the story of what had happened to them. The morning of the bombings, Laurel and Sue had slept in about 15 minutes. Then Sue, Laurel, and Fran went out on the street to catch a cab to go to the subway. They couldn't find a cab and soon they heard about what had happened. They missed being on the subway by about 15 minutes. Sometimes it's alright to sleep in.

Post Scriptum: I should warn you about being with Uncle Fran. When he went to Rome the Pope died. When he went to London – they blew it up!

8

Clarence and the Truck

Between 1977 and 1983 I worked for a general construction company named Rapid Plumbing. Rapid Plumbing was owned by Clarence Harrison who had gone to the South Dakota School of Mines on a basketball scholarship and graduated as a Mechanical Engineer in the early 1950s. I went to High School with his son Kenny and daughter Jeannie. I played football with Kenny who dated Cathy Callahan on my Swim team.

Rapid Plumbing was originally a plumbing and heating/ air conditioning company but Clarence expanded it until we did concrete, masonry, steel work, landscaping, carpentry, and about everything it took to put up large commercial buildings worth up to about one or two million dollars in the late 1970s. I don't think he wanted to get much larger than that because it would risk his capital. It was also quite a job keeping all his men working year around because he felt quite responsible for us. As I look back on him now I see that he was a good boss and very fair. He worked right alongside of us and I think he enjoyed physical labor as he was very athletic as a young man. In Sturgis, South Dakota he led his high school basketball team to the state championship and he quarterbacked his football team (from the fullback position). One of Clarence's sons told me the kids of his high school had wanted Clarence to play pro football.

When I knew him he seemed like a tough old man.

In about 1980 Rapid Plumbing had about 30 different men working for it. There was my foreman George Maher, an outstanding brick mason who could lay more units a day than anyone else I ever saw. There were the two Marks, the masons, and me the main masonry tender. Then there were various equipment operators, plumbers, sheet metal workers, laborers, foremen, etc. One particularly notable man was Ward Ham. Ward had been a Sargent in the Marine Corps during World War II and been a sniper/scout. He told of being sent ashore before the bombardments of the beaches would start. He was another tough, tough man. I just don't see many men of the caliber of Ward and Clarence and George when I look around. George would work hard all day at Rapid Plumbing and then work at night and on weekends to support his family doing odd jobs that he would pick up. I don't remember hearing a lot of complaining about the unfairness of the country from those men either. They worked hard and made a good living.

At Rapid Plumbing the foremen would need to carry a lot of tools from job to job on company trucks. Somehow Sue got the ridiculous notion in her mind that Clarence should give me a truck. I tried to explain that only foremen got trucks or special people like Clarence's son Kenny. Well that didn't seem to satisfy Sue so she got to praying. At that time we only had one car but we had three kids. If Sue needed the car she would take me to work at 6:30 in the morning. Sometimes she needed the car for carpooling the kids to the Christian school the kids were going to.

One day at a hanger we were building out at the airport, Clarence motioned for me to come over. He said, "John, is that the only car you have?"

I said, "Yes."

He said, "What does your wife think about that?"

I said, "There's not much she can think about it."

He said, "I'm giving you Ward's truck."

Then later on I went out to the office and he sold me the truck for a dollar. I didn't have a dollar on me. He gave me the dollar. God gave me that truck in answer to my wife's prayer.

9

Jesus Comes to Our House

I don't really know what to make of this next story. I didn't hear about it until I was about 56 or so and so it seems very questionable to me. I've asked my mom about it several times and she never tells me she was just kidding.

My dad was quite sickly. Other dads played sports with their kids but my dad never did with me. We never went camping. I went fishing one time with him when I was maybe in grade school. When I was little Dad hunted a lot and when he moved to Sioux Falls in 1974 he started hunting again, but never with me.

When he was about 11 or twelve years old he had osteomyeolitis which is a bone disease in his legs. The bones in his feet were fused together and he couldn't walk that well. That is why he was 4 F during WWII. Strangely he loved to dance and he and Mom would swing dance – I don't know how. Mom said he would like to drink a little and perhaps that relieved some of his pain so he could move better. I never saw my dad take a drink in my life.

Then in the 50s he had his gall bladder removed and started to have serious operations every couple of years. I was just a little boy and Alice was younger so we never knew what was going on. I remember visiting him in the hospital.

One time Dad was having an operation and we were living in Rapid City so it was after 1962. Mom was worried sick. Laurel was away at college, Nancy was in high school, Alice and I were in grade school. There was a knock at the door.

Jesus was at the door and asked to come in.

He came in and sat in our living room.

He told Mom, "Don't worry, everything will be all right."

Then He left.

Everything was all right.

10

God Raises the Dead

The Bible records many unusual things. One of the foundations of Chritianity is our belief in the resurrection of the dead. Many Protestants have an empty cross in their church to show them that Jesus rose from the dead. I tend to be more like the Catholic Church in that regard in that I like the reminder that Jesus died for my sins on the cross so I like to see Jesus on the cross.

The resurrection of Jesus is not the only resurrection from the dead recorded in the Bible. Elijah raised up a little boy and so did Elisha. A dead man came back to life who fell on Elisha's bones. Lazarus was raised to life and so was the son of the widow from Nain.

When I was a young Christian in about 1971 I read a book called *Like a Mighty Wind* by Mel Tari where Mel tells the story of raising someone from the dead. I however had never had any personal contact with people that were raised from the dead.

That is no longer true.

I have personally talked to three people that have been raised from the dead and have been part of one of those events. In Brother Branham's ministry there were several documented cases that I am aware of: a boy in Finland, a baby in Mexico, Brother Way, and several others. I talked with Brother Way.

Brother Way was a missionary in Africa who met and married Sister Way another missionary. They used to follow Brother Branham from place to place in the United States and finally ended up in Minot, ND where we got to know them in Rapid City, SD. Brother Way had been healed of Malaria in Brother Branham's meetings and during the 1960s he and Sister Way were at a meeting in Jeffersonville, IN. At the close of the meeting, during the song service, Brother Way had a fatal heart attack. His eyes rolled back and he collapsed. I have listened to the tape of this service and you can hear this all happening.

Brother Branham came down and prayed for Brother Way and he recovered.

A second incident that I was not involved in occurred with a Sister in Sioux Fall, SD. Brother Calvin Honeycutt moved from Indiana and started a small house church. His wife was from the area and her sister came to the church. When the sister was a little girl she had gotten trapped behind the bed and smothered and turned blue and died. Their father had begun to pray and cry in desperation before God. God heard their prayers and life came back into the little girl.

The third event I will never forget. It occurred in Rapid City on a Sunday night or Wednesday night. We had just gotten out of church and people were gathered on the steps of our little church and around the base of the steps. I believe I was on the top of the steps.

It was dark. We were talking and friendly and milling about.

Then I heard:

BANG!

BANG!

My head seemed to see a white object flying through the street about thirty feet in front of me and going south toward the corner. But this happened in a flash. I remember Larry Sietsema in the street directing traffic around.

Little Amanda Ovitt had been struck by a car traveling the speed limit. She had darted out between parked cars and the driver hadn't seen her and the first bang was when she was knocked into the air and the second bang knocked her about 25 or 30 feet. Physics tells us a one hundred pound girl versus a two ton vehicle doesn't stand a chance. We had two nurses in our congregation, Lynn Clark and Naomi Rosenkrantz, -- one of them tried to find a pulse without any luck. Then Doug Christiansen, a former airman tried again with no success. Then we gathered for prayer.

I remember my thoughts at the time as we laid hands on the still form, "Why are we even praying, she is dead."

Doug prayed, "Lord Jesus –" and I have forgotten the rest of the prayer but Jesus heard our prayers. A while later I was back on the steps and I heard moaning and an ambulance had come and Amanda was alive.

I have met three people that God has raised from the dead. And someday, if Jesus tarries I hope to be one of those that He raises from the dead too.

I was standing on the steps even with the street.
Amanda was knocked even with the building to the
intersection where we prayed for her in the street.

11

Brother Joe and Sister Teresa

I have purposely kept this book up until now mostly personal with a few exceptions like Marylou's godly grandfather. Now I want to share some of the stories of friends of mine from church.

I go to a little church of about 70 people in East Troy, Wisconsin called the House of the Lord pastored by Michael Braund. Brother Mike is a former Catholic who owns a printing business and is a prison evangelist who has been in dozens of prisons from Florida to Minnesota. I have been with him in Tennessee and Wisconsin dozens of times. Our congregation has Hispanics, whites, and blacks – everyone is welcome.

When Brother Mike got saved, his wife and many of her siblings got saved also including Sarah. Sarah had a son Bob. Bob had a friend named Joe. Brother Joe.

Brother Joe was a biker. Brother Joe was married to a biker chick named Teresa. They were not saved. They were definitely not saved.

As God began dealing in Bob's life he felt a burden for his friend Joe. At that time Bob had some tapes of a ministry of Brother William Branham that he felt led to share with Joe. So he played a tape for Joe. Joe didn't like it at all. But he liked Bob. And then he couldn't get the tape out of his mind so after a while he brought Teresa to church and they got saved.

Now Joe and Teresa had been married for quite a while and couldn't have children. The doctors told them they couldn't have children. At church they were prayed over to have children.

Sister Teresa took it to heart. Brother Joe thought she was nuts!! She started to get the baby's room ready – just like she was going to have a baby – what a nut job!

Then, she was pregnant and they had Samuel!

Then, she was pregnant and they had Jacob!

Then—she was pregnant and they had Daniel!

Then—she was pregnant and they had Naomi!

When I am sick I want to have Brother Joe and Sister Teresa pray for me. I feel like I am in the presence of Abraham and Sarah when I am around them.

Brother Joe, Teresa, Samuel, Daniel, Jacob, and Naomi

12

Sister Donna's Dad

At our church we pray for anybody. They don't have to come to our church and they don't have to believe what we believe. It amazes me the results that simple prayer gets. A case is Sister Donna's Dad. Donna and Andrew Rimner have six tall beautiful blond daughters.

I am six foot 3 ½ inches tall and Brother Andrew towers over me like Goliath over David. My hand is small inside his. Sister Donna is about 5 foot 8 or so. My wife Susan is five ten so Donna isn't as tall as Sue (This is a different Donna from the Donna of the chickens). Sister Donna has a Father who doesn't come to our church and was diagnosed with prostate cancer with a PST of 9 and given a few months to live.

A prayer request came in. Our church prayed. Each week it seemed like the diagnosis changed a little bit until the last I heard he had arthritis, no cancer and a PST of 1. Now it is my understanding that a PST of 1 is better than normal.

After prayer is made and a miracle occurs we are always tempted to say it was a coincidence or it would have happened anyway. In my experience I have noticed that after prayer there is a remarkable amount of positive "coincidences" that "coincide" with our prayers. I am not ashamed to give My heavenly Father the glory and thanks He deserves for hearing our prayers and answering them.

Sister Donna's Dad

Donna and Daughters Abby, Brianna, Michelle, and Hannah

13

Jackie's Miracle Baby

The last story I want to share is about my niece Jackie. Jackie is Uncle Fran's daughter. I often joke that we only allow beautiful women to join our family, but if you should ever see Jackie you would know what I mean.

Jackie had three children in her first marriage, Dominic, Mitch, and Alexa. Then she married Greg. Greg is a great guy that comes from a Cincinnati family that is all about family. He loves Jackie's first three kids and has a good time with our whole family at our Thanksgiving celebration in Milwaukee.

In the spring of 2013 we were all excited because Jackie and Greg were going to have a baby! Our excitement turned to concern as we learned that the baby had a tumor.

During the spring and summer of 2013 we got ultrasound pictures of the baby and found out she was a baby girl that was to be named Courtney Grace. Our Church went to praying. People were praying for little Courtney Grace in Cincinnati. I'm sure my niece's Methodist Church in

Wahpeton, North Dakota was praying as well as First United Methodist church in Sioux Falls, SD where Nancy, Mark and my mother attend. Then there is Luther Seminary in Minneapolis St.Paul where my niece Christy and her fiancé Jon attend and World Wide Revival Church in Kansas City, Missouri. When Jackie's last few weeks of pregnancy were upon her and Courtney Grace there were believers in Ohio, Kentucky, Wisconsin, Minnesota, North Dakota, South Dakota, and Missouri praying for the safety of an unborn innocent baby and her mother.

Jackie couldn't go to work and because of the danger to both her and the baby she stayed largely in bed in the hospital. When the day came for the baby to be delivered by caesarian section the tumor had grown to over four pounds and was joined to little Courtney Grace's bottom.

Pictures of Courtney Grace show a growth like a large gourd attached to her that was similar in size to another child but not viable lacking the necessary organs for life. Within several days the growth was separated from Courtney Grace and all that remained was an M shaped incision that the surgeon carefully stitched closed. What a miracle!

Many might look at this story and only see modern science and medicine. My family sees the God that used modern science and medicine to answer the prayers of believing Catholics, Lutherans, Methodists, Pentecostals, Evangelicals, Message Believers and others.

14

The Miracles Continue

There are many other stories and miracles I could write about and someday perhaps I will. Alice would like to tell about the motorcycle and the bills. There is Brother Don and the white Cow. I could tell about how I got married in ten days. You get the idea. When you spend time with God and His people you will find that you are surrounded by miracles.

John Wheeldon would like to continue teaching until they unwrap his cold, dead, tired fingers from around a piece of chalk. At one time, John had tried out careers in carpentry, masonry, truck driving, manufacturing, etc., but, due to a lack of talent, decided to become an engineer.

He loves his students at the Milwaukee School of Engineering because they are at a delightful time of life and generally want to learn electrical engineering from him. Of course, if he earns so much income from writing that he and overworked but much-appreciated wife, Susan, are forced to take trips to exotic locales to research upcoming books, they will reluctantly make that sacrifice (sigh).

John and Sue grew up in the beautiful Black Hills of South Dakota but now live in New Berlin, Wisconsin, a suburb of Milwaukee. They have four adult children and nine incredibly handsome, beautiful, and intelligent grandchildren whom they enjoy visiting and watching football, soccer, violin, baseball, and dance.